SAN FRANCISCO

MICHAEL E. GOODMAN

THE HISTORY OF THE
GIANTS

40

CREATIVE EDUCATION

Published by Creative Education
123 South Broad Street, Mankato, Minnesota 56001
Creative Education is an imprint of The Creative Company

Designed by Rita Marshall
Editorial assistance by Julie Bach & John Nichols

Photos by: Allsport Photography, Archive Photos, Corbis-Bettmann, Focus on
Sports, Fotosport, SportsChrome.

Library of Congress Cataloging-in-Publication Data

Goodman, Michael.
The History of the San Francisco Giants / by Michael Goodman.
p. cm. — (Baseball)
Summary: A team history of the Giants, who arrived in San Francisco in 1958
from New York, where they had played for 75 years, thrilling fans on both
coasts.
ISBN: 0-88682-924-0

1. San Francisco Giants (Baseball team)—History—Juvenile literature.
[1. San Francisco Giants (Baseball team)—History. 2. Baseball—History.]
I. Title. II. Series: Baseball (Mankato, Minn.)

GV875.S34G66 1999
796.357'64'0979461—dc21   97-6341

First edition

9 8 7 6 5 4 3 2 1

Some people say that no city in the United States is as beautiful and exciting as San Francisco, California. The city sits atop a series of steep hills, surrounded on three sides by water and connected to the rest of California by two well-known bridges—the Golden Gate and the San Francisco–Oakland Bay Bridge. Strong winds and thick fog often sweep across these bridges and over the city, adding an air of mystery to its dramatic beauty.

One place where the winds blow strongest is San Francisco's Candlestick Park, the stadium where the San Francisco Giants have been playing baseball since 1960. Two years

Hall-of-Famer Bill Terry.

before Candlestick Park opened, the club was moved across the country from its former home in New York City.

The Giants brought to the West Coast a long tradition of playing hard-nosed, winning baseball. San Francisco's fans already knew about such great Giants stars of the past as Christy Mathewson, Frankie Frisch, Bill Terry, Mel Ott, Carl Hubbell, Bobby Thomson, and Sal Maglie. Soon they had their own Giants heroes, including Willie Mays, Willie McCovey, Juan Marichal, and father-and-son combination Bobby and Barry Bonds. Twice since 1958 the Giants have come close to moving again, but for now it looks as if their fans will continue to enjoy professional baseball. In fact, the Giants are planning to build a new ballpark, to be named Pacific Bell Park, in time for Opening Day in the year 2000. The first game in the stadium will mark the beginning of a new chapter in the century-old franchise's history—a history that began on a deserted polo field in New York and now lives on in the city by the bay.

Buck Ewing, who was later inducted into the Hall of Fame (1939), became a founding member of the New York Giants.

MUTRIE'S BIG FELLOWS PERFORM

The Giants began their National League history in New York City in 1883, 75 years before their move to San Francisco. In those days the club was known by several names such as the "Gothams" or "Nationals." The team played their home games just north of New York's Central Park in an area that had been used for polo matches. Thus the field was referred to as the Polo Grounds. The same name was later given to a new baseball stadium built a little farther uptown.

Rising star pitcher Shawn Estes.

Joe McGinnity established two season records that still stand today: most complete games (44) and most innings (434).

New York was among the top teams in its league. They were led on both offense and defense by Buck Ewing, the best catcher of his era and the first player in the 19th century to earn more than $5,000 a year. New York fans loved to watch Ewing play, and he enjoyed showing off for them. During one game, he led off the top of the 10th inning with a single and proceeded to steal second and third bases. Standing on third, Ewing turned to the crowd and shouted, "It's getting late. I'm going to steal home, and then we can all have dinner." A few pitches later, Buck slid safely across home plate, and everyone headed home.

The Nationals' manager, James Mutrie, was clearly proud of Ewing and his other stars. As the players headed to or from the bench, he would cheer them on by shouting, "Come on, my big fellows, my giants!" A New York sportswriter heard Mutrie and started using the nickname in his stories. By 1885, Giants had became the official team name. The Giants won back-to-back National League pennants in 1888 and 1889, but then faded to the middle of the league standings until the beginning of the 20th century. That was when a tough Irishman named John McGraw took control of the club and launched what has been called the Giants' golden era.

ONLY ONE MANAGER—JOHN McGRAW

When 28-year-old John McGraw arrived in New York late in 1902, the Giants were at a low point. The team was in last place, far behind the league-leading Pittsburgh Pirates. Under McGraw's leadership, and behind the pitching talents of Joe McGinnity and Christy Mathewson, the club finished a solid second in the standings in 1903 and then first in both 1904 and 1905.

McGinnity was called "Iron Man" because he never seemed to get tired. Three times in August of 1903, he hurled both games of doubleheaders and won all six contests. McGinnity's iron arm helped him record 31 wins in 1903 and 35 in 1904.

As good as McGinnity was, Mathewson was even better. Combining a rocket fastball and a sweeping curve with an unusual pitch called a "fadeaway" (known as a screwball today), Mathewson proceeded to mow down National League batters at a record pace for more than a dozen years. He finished his career with 373 victories and more than 2,500 strikeouts. "There never was any pitcher like Mathewson," McGraw said. "And I doubt there ever will be."

McGraw pushed players like McGinnity and Mathewson—and later such New York stars as Frankie Frisch, George Kelly, Casey Stengel, and Ross Youngs—and brought out the best in them. He was a dictator on the field. "The main idea," he always said, "is to win." And that's exactly what the Giants did. During McGraw's 31 years at the helm (1902–1932), the Giants captured 10 pennants and finished in second place 11 times.

During one amazing stretch in the early 1920s, the Giants won four straight National League titles. They also recorded back-to-back World Series triumphs over Babe Ruth's Yankees in 1921 and 1922 and came within one out of winning a third championship against the Washington Senators in the 1924 World Series.

1 9 0 8

In a fine season, Christy Mathewson led the Giants' pitching staff with 37 victories.

Slugging third baseman Matt Williams.

1989 NL MVP Kevin Mitchell.

Throughout his career, McGraw was both feared and respected by his players and his opponents. As the legendary Connie Mack once said, "There has been only one manager, and his name is John McGraw."

"MEMPHIS BILL," "MASTER MELVIN," AND "KING CARL"

1 9 2 9

In only his fourth full season with the Giants, Mel Ott established a club record by driving in 151 runs.

Though McGraw didn't win any pennants in his last few seasons with the Giants, he did develop three players who would lead the team back to the top of the National League in the 1930s—Bill Terry, Mel Ott, and Carl Hubbell.

Terry, a lanky first baseman from Memphis, Tennessee, was a remarkable hitter. He had a lifetime batting average of .341 and was the last National League batter to hit more than .400 in a season. Terry was also the best fielding first baseman of his era. Then in 1932, he took on added responsibility when McGraw asked him to become the team's manager.

The new player/manager took over a team that had finished in sixth place in 1932, but he was certain the club would bounce back. "We'll do third or better," he told writers. Why was Terry so confident? He knew he had two of the best hitters in the league—Mel Ott and himself—and the best pitcher in "King Carl" Hubbell.

Ott had first joined the Giants in 1926 when he was only 17 years old, so some writers called him "Master Melvin." He had one of the strangest batting styles of all time. As a pitch came toward the plate, the left-handed Ott lifted his right foot, and then shifted his weight forward to snap his bat at the ball.

Some of the Giants' coaches wanted to change Ott's style, but McGraw wouldn't let them. "Do what's comfortable for you," McGraw told his young star. Once again McGraw was proved right. He knew Ott's swing was perfect for the short 257-foot right-field fence in the Polo Grounds. By the time Master Melvin retired in 1947, he had become only the third player in major-league history to hit more than 500 homers (511). The other two were Babe Ruth and Jimmy Foxx.

The third part of Bill Terry's winning plan in 1933 was the left-handed Hubbell, who had the most unhittable screwball since Christy Mathewson. Tying National League batters in knots throughout the 1930s, Hubbell went on to win 253 games, a total second only to that of Mathewson in Giants history. Hubbell also had terrific control. In 1933, Hubbell pitched all 18 innings of a crucial game against St. Louis. Not only did he win the game 1–0, but he didn't walk a single batter and struck out 12. To this date, there has never been a performance to match that one.

1 9 3 2

Besides directing the Giants to the NL championship, Bill Terry also led the club with 225 hits.

Hubbell, Ott, and Terry had such great seasons in 1933 that the Giants surpassed Terry's expectations, finishing in first place. The team was practically unstoppable, defeating the Washington Senators in the 1933 World Series four games to one.

The trio of New York stars also led the Giants to National League titles in 1936 and 1937. Then age began to take its toll on the trio of stars, and the club sank to the middle of the league standings, where it remained throughout the 1940s.

"MIRACLES" AND THE "SAY HEY KID"

As the 1950s began, Giants fans were longing for another winner at the Polo Grounds. They got their wish in

In the All-Star Game, Carl Hubbell struck out Ruth, Gehrig, Foxx, Simmons, and Cronin—a remarkable feat.

1951 when the Giants staged one of the greatest comebacks in National League history. In early August, New York trailed the Brooklyn Dodgers by a huge 13½ game margin. Then the Giants got hot, winning 37 of their last 44 contests. New York slowly crept up on its crosstown rival, and the two teams finished the season in a dead heat. They then faced off in a special best-of-three-games playoff to decide who would claim the National League pennant.

New York won game one on a Bobby Thomson home run. Brooklyn tied the series with a 10–0 blowout in game two. In the third and final contest, Brooklyn held a 4–1 lead in the bottom of the ninth inning. Giants fans were worried, but they got some encouragement when New York rallied for one run and had base-runners on second and third with only one out.

Up stepped Thomson, the hero of the first playoff game. Dodgers manager Charlie Dressen brought in star pitcher Ralph Branca to face Thomson. Branca tried to slip a high, inside fastball past the Giants' batter, but the right-handed slugger stepped back from the plate as he swung and sent the ball sailing over the left-field stands for a three-run homer. As Thomson circled the bases, New York's radio announcer Russ Hodges began screaming into his microphone, "The Giants win the pennant! The Giants win the pennant! They're going crazy! Ooooh, boy!" Giants fans will always remember that home run. The dramatic victory would come to be known as "the Miracle of Coogan's Bluff," which was the location of the Polo Grounds.

A second miracle occurred in Coogan's Bluff just three years later, after New York had won another National League

Slick-fielding shortstop Jose Uribe.

16   *All-time great Willie Mays.*

pennant. The Giants were taking on the favored Cleveland Indians in game one of the 1954 World Series. This time the hero was New York's 23-year-old center fielder Willie "Say Hey" Mays. With the score tied 2–2 in the top of the eighth inning and two Indian runners on base, Cleveland slugger Vic Wertz sent a mammoth drive to the deepest part of center field in the Polo Grounds. It seemed certain the blast would sail over Mays' head and win the game for Cleveland. But Mays turned his back to home plate and raced to where he thought the ball would come down. He judged the catch perfectly and grabbed the ball over his shoulder on a dead run. Then he whirled around and threw back to the infield to hold the runners in place. Cleveland never recovered from that play. The Giants rallied to win game one in extra innings and then swept the next three contests from the brokenhearted Indians.

Under manager Bill Rigney, the Giants finished their first season in San Francisco in third place.

The jovial Mays was as popular off the field as he was great on it. The amiable slugger loved to talk with writers and fans, but he had a terrible time remembering names. Mays would playfully hide his problem by using the all-purpose greeting "Say hey." Teammate Monte Irvin joked, "I think Willie remembers his mom's name, but everybody else is 'Say Hey.'" Before long, Mays became known as the "Say Hey Kid." Giants fans in New York and later in San Francisco also grew to know Mays by the magic he worked in the field and at bat. Many baseball experts consider him to be the greatest all-around player in the game's history. Said Leo Durocher, his longtime manager, "If somebody came up and hit .450, stole 100 bases, and performed a miracle on the field every day, I'd look you in the eye and say that Willie

Gold Glove-winning first baseman Will Clark (pages 18-19).

was better. He could do the five things you have to do to be a superstar: hit, hit with power, run, throw, and field. And he had another magic ingredient. . . . He lit up the room when he came in. He was a joy to be around."

Unfortunately for New York fans, they got to watch Mays perform for only a few years. By the start of the 1958 season, the Giants had moved to their new home in San Francisco.

1 9 6 6

With 25 wins, Juan Marichal recorded more than 20 victories for the fourth consecutive season.

MAYS, McCOVEY, AND MARICHAL SHINE

When the Giants first arrived in San Francisco, local fans knew few of the players except Willie Mays, but they turned out in record numbers to cheer for their new heroes. Mays had no trouble adjusting to the sun and winds of Northern California. In his first year on the West Coast, the multitalented Mays batted .347, hit 29 homers, drove in 96 runs, and led the league in runs scored (121) and stolen bases (31). Yet when the fans voted for Most Valuable Giant in 1958, Mays came in second to rookie sensation Orlando Cepeda. The San Francisco fans always had a special feeling for Cepeda, because he was the first Giants star who began his career in the "City by the Bay."

The next year, fans had another "home-grown" hero to cheer for—Willie "Stretch" McCovey. San Franciscans knew McCovey would be someone special from the first night he put on a Giants uniform. The 6-foot-4 slugger tripled his first time at bat and finished the game with two triples and two singles. Even though he played only 52 games in 1959, he was easily elected National League Rookie of the Year. When veteran pitcher Lew Burdette of the Braves was asked which pitch McCovey could hit best, he replied, "He hits curves, sliders, and fastballs—everything I can throw at him."

Mays, Cepeda, and McCovey were soon joined in San Francisco by a young hurler from the Dominican Republic named Juan Marichal. Marichal had three things a great pitcher needs: speed, control, and confidence. He put all three to work the first time he took the mound in 1960. Facing the Philadelphia Phillies, Marichal had a no-hitter going until catcher Clay Dalrymple singled with two outs in the eighth inning for Philadelphia's only hit.

John "The Count" Montefusco struck out 215 batters on his way to winning the Rookie of the Year award.

After the game, writers swarmed around the young pitcher, who could speak only a few words of English. Cepeda served as translator. A reporter asked, "Were you surprised at how well you performed today?"

"He says, 'No,'" Cepeda reported. "'I expected to win. I always expect to win.'" By the time he finished his Hall of Fame career, Marichal had registered 243 wins and more than 2,300 strikeouts.

With their talent and confidence, the Giants returned to the top of the National League. San Francisco won the pennant in 1962 and battled the Yankees evenly in the 1962 World Series. They trailed 1–0 going into the bottom of the ninth inning of game seven. Then the Giants got two runners on base, with McCovey coming to bat. As San Francisco fans stood and screamed, Stretch hit a scorcher right at Yankees second baseman Bobby Richardson. If the ball had been just a few inches to the right or left, the Giants would have won the game and the series. But it was not to be.

The Giants began a decline in the early 1970s as aging stars Mays and McCovey were traded to other teams and

The incomparable Robby Thompson.

Marichal was released. Young players such as Bobby Bonds, Dave Kingman, Gary Matthews, Jack Clark, and John "The Count" Montefusco arrived to take their places, but the Giants' winning magic was gone. The team would not seriously challenge again for the remainder of the decade.

THE GREAT TURNAROUND BEGINS

1 9 8 . 9

Scott Garrelts, moved from the bullpen to the starting rotation, led the NL in ERA and winning percentage.

The Giants started losing regularly in the late 1970s and early 1980s, and fewer fans came to the games at Candlestick Park. Team owner Bob Lurie threatened to sell the franchise or move it to a different city. Lurie's threats upset the fans and the players, both of whom pinned their hopes on the Giants' new manager, Roger Craig, and the new general manager, Al Rosen, who took charge of the club in 1986. These two men led the team to a stunning turnaround. "We're going to get back to the basics," Craig announced. "If we can discipline ourselves to do the little things right, the big things will take care of themselves."

Rosen also got into the act by promoting three fairly young infielders—Will Clark, Robby Thompson, and Jose Uribe—to the Giants' squad and trading for outfielder Candy Maldonado. Clark earned his nickname, "The Thrill," right away. He homered in his first time at bat in the majors against Houston in the Astrodome, and hit another home run in his first game at Candlestick a week later. The Giants and their young star were on their way.

By the time the 1986 season ended, San Francisco had won 83 games (21 more than in 1985) and had jumped from last place to third in the NL West. Nearly 700,000 more fans

Third baseman Matt Williams drove in 122 runs to lead the National League for the season.

attended home games than during the previous year. For the time being, there was no more talk of moving the franchise.

"It's nice to win some games, but the Giants won't rest until we win the big one," stated Craig. The team came close to reaching its goal in 1987, capturing its first NL West title since 1971. Then the Giants took the St. Louis Cardinals to a seventh game in the National League Championship Series before losing the pennant and a shot at the World Series.

Two years later, however, San Francisco was back. Behind Clark and his new teammate, slugging outfielder Kevin Mitchell, the Giants swept to another NL West title. Up next would be the Chicago Cubs in the National League Championship Series, and this time the Giants were ready. San Francisco pounded the Cubs four games to one to advance to their first World Series in 27 years. Their opponent in the fall classic would be the Giants' neighbor across the bay, the powerful Oakland A's.

Baseball experts expected an exciting World Series, but no one could have predicted the dramatic event that took place in October 1989. After Oakland won the first two games in its home park, the series moved to Candlestick. Half an hour before game three was to begin, a devastating earthquake shook the Bay Area. Baseball became a secondary concern that night as players and fans huddled together in the stadium and said prayers of thanks for being alive. Ten days later the series resumed, and Oakland completed a four-game sweep of the Giants. San Francisco fans were disappointed, but the earthquake tragedy added perspective. "We lost a few baseball games, but a lot of people lost a lot more," said shaken pitcher Atlee Hammaker.

24

After making it all the way to the World Series, the Giants entered a slide that left them a whopping 26 games behind the Atlanta Braves, the division champion, in 1992. Rumors circulated that the Giants might move to Florida, but once again San Francisco fans were spared. A group headed by businessman Peter Magowan stepped forward and purchased the team in December 1992. Magowan named a new general manager, Bob Quinn, and a new manager, Dusty Baker, in hopes of bringing the sleeping Giants back to life. He also thrilled the fans by signing Hall-of-Famer Willie Mays to a lifetime contract with the team's front office. But of all the new additions, one in particular gave Giants fans the most hope. Two-time league MVP left fielder Barry Bonds, son of Bobby Bonds and godson of Willie Mays, signed a six-year contract to continue the family business: winning baseball games for the Giants.

1 9 9 3

John Burkett's 22 victories for the Giants put him at the top of the National League.

Magowan's moves paid off. The team sizzled through the 1993 campaign, winning 103 games while losing only 59. "Usually 100 wins is more than enough to get it done," sighed Baker, the 1993 Manager of the Year. "But 1993 was one crazy year." Incredibly, the Giants finished one game behind the division-leading Atlanta Braves in one of the great season-long races of all time. "That team [the Giants] won't get any reward for what they've done," said Braves manager Bobby Cox. "It's a shame, because that's a heckuva team."

The Giants' success that year was built on a strong roster of players, including third baseman Matt Williams, who

Smooth-fielding, hard-hitting J. T. Snow (pages 26-27).

A good batting eye, combined with careful opposing pitchers, led to a Giants-record 151 walks for Barry Bonds.

boasted a .294 average, 38 homers, and 110 RBIs. Robby Thompson celebrated career highs of a .312 average, 19 home runs, and 65 RBIs. Darren Lewis set a major-league record by playing 267 consecutive errorless games in center field. The Giants' pitching staff showed strength as well. It featured baseball's best closer that year, Rod Beck, who recorded 48 saves, and John Burkett and Bill Swift, the team's first two 20-game winners since 1966.

But perhaps the biggest Giant that year was Barry Bonds. Bonds batted .336 with 46 home runs, 123 RBIs, and 29 stolen bases. His efforts were enough to claim a third Most Valuable Player Award, tying the league's all-time record.

Bonds, who had grown up on the West Coast, had been playing in Pittsburgh up until 1992 when he left for free agency. He signed with San Francisco for a whopping $43.5 million contract for six years, a price tag that raised the fans' expectations—perhaps to unrealistic heights. Bonds was criticized in the 1995 strike-shortened season when he hit .294, banged 33 home runs, and had 104 RBIs. A career year for most major-leaguers was a disappointment for arguably the game's best player. "People expect a lot from me," explained Bonds. "But nobody expects more than I do."

Bonds and the Giants came back to exceed all expectations in 1997 when they captured the NL West crown after being picked by most experts to finish in last place. Again, Bonds led the way, shaking off a slow start to crunch 40 homers, knock in 101 runs and steal 37 bases. The Giants would lose to the eventual World Series champion Florida Marlins in the first round of the postseason, but for Baker, the season was still special. "This team didn't have a lot of stars, but they played together and never gave up," remarked the manager. "We've got a lot of character to build on."

GIANT POTENTIAL FOR SUCCESS

Jeff Kent did heavy damage from the cleanup spot, batting .316 and crushing 29 home runs.

The heart the Giants showed in 1997 will be counted on heavily for the team's future success. "We've got strong veteran leaders like Barry [Bonds], Jeff Kent, and J.T Snow in our clubhouse," said Baker. "With competitors like that, I see us being a big factor in any race."

Kent and Snow joined the Giants in separate trades before the 1997 season, and both players made an immediate impact in San Francisco. The scrappy yet powerful second baseman Kent brings a strong bat and a combative attitude to the Giants. His 29 home runs and 121 RBIs in 1997 gave the team a taste of seasons yet to come from the former member of the New York Mets and Cleveland Indians. "Jeff's hyper and strong-willed," said Bonds with a smile. "You better be ready to play as hard as he does or he'll get in your face. Even mine."

The graceful first baseman Snow survived a scary spring training beaning by Seattle Mariners fireballer Randy Johnson to go on to a monster 1997 season. His 28 homers and 104 RBIs were both career highs for Snow, who had previously played for the Anaheim Angels. "J.T has always been a fantastic fielder, but what he's shown us with the bat has been outstanding," said Baker. "He's just coming into his own, and we're very excited about it."

Perhaps the Giants' brightest young star is left-handed pitcher Shawn Estes. The 24-year-old turned in a stellar '97

Kirk Rueter, a standout pitcher.

One of baseball's greatest—Barry Bonds.

Manager Dusty Baker, with two Manager of the Year awards (1993 and 1997), was driving his team to the top.

season, posting a 19–5 record with 181 strikeouts and a 3.18 ERA. "This kid's got a real competitor's heart," said pitching coach Dick Pole. "I keep telling myself he's just a kid, but on the mound he's a 10-year vet." Estes looks to team with fellow young lefty Kirk Rueter and veteran Mark Gardner to form a solid rotation in San Francisco for years to come. In the bullpen, newly acquired closer Rob Nen gives the Giants a late-inning stopper who, with help from Julian Tavarez and Doug Henry, should succeed in that role.

With Bonds (possibly the game's most dynamic player) in place to lead them on the field and Baker (one of baseball's sharpest minds) to guide them from the bench, the Giants look to be building something special again. "I know for a fact that these guys are just starting to figure out how good they can be," explained Baker. "I'm excited about our future." With a new stadium on the way and a contending team already built, Giants fans hope to enjoy a future as promising as the team's glorious past.